just

the Caravaggio

Anne MacLeod

POETRY SALZBURG
at the University of Salzburg

SALZBURG - OXFORD – PORTLAND

1999

First published in 1999 by **POETRY SALZBURG** at the University of
Salzburg

EDITOR: WOLFGANG GÖRTSCHACHER
EDITORIAL ASSISTANT: ANDREAS SCHACHERMAYR

ISBN: 3-901993-00-2

INSTITUT FÜR ANGLISTIK UND AMERIKANISTIK
UNIVERSITÄT SALZBURG
AKADEMIESTR. 24
A-5020 SALZBURG
AUSTRIA

Distributed by
Drake International Services
Market House, Market Place,
Deddington, Oxford OX15 0SF
England
Phone 01869 338240
Fax: 01869 338310

Distributed in the U.S.A. by
International Specialised Book Services Inc.
5804 NE Hassalo Street
Portland
Oregon 97213-3644
Phone 503.287.3093
Fax: 503.280.8832

for Joanne

CONTENTS

I TRACE YOUR NAME

ANGEL GRAVESTONES

ACKNOWLEDGEMENTS

Grateful acknowledgements to the editors of the following magazines in which some of these poems first appeared, sometimes in earlier versions;

Aberdeen University Review, The Arvon Journal, The Poet's Voice, Poetry Scotland, The Swansea Review, West Coast Magazine, West Highland Free Press; also to *Present Poets*, a National Museums of Scotland anthology, and *After the Watergaw* (WaterAid/Scottish Cultural Press).

I would like to thank the Scottish Arts Council for making it possible for me to attend the 1996 *Poetry in the Making* conference at the University of Salzburg, which proved such a wonderful, stimulating experience. I am grateful to Iain Crichton Smith for his poetry, *The Thoughts of Murdo*, and his introduction to this volume. Iain's recent death is a great loss to the world and to us all.

I owe many thanks to my editors, James Hogg and Wolfgang Görtschacher for their kindness and enthusiasm; also to Peter Mortimer for letting me borrow his elegant 'The extreme of white': further thanks are due to Pete, and to Linda Anderson and Tom Bryan for their early reading of this manuscript and their encouragement and gently-offered advice.

To Jim, who underpins it all, my love.

PREFACE

One could say, I think, that Anne MacLeod has decided on her style. It is a style often uninterrupted by punctuation: and this gives it a sense of excitement and rush which a more lapidary style wouldn't. It also gives it an openness to experience.

For the most part, though not entirely, this is an openness to experience to nature (more so in this new book). There is reference to rivers, to apples, to owls. One would expect this because of the area where the author lives, and her background. I suppose the fascination with rivers in the first part of the book again suits her style of forward movement and clarity. There is also much about snow, frost and trees.

However, it isn't all poetry about nature: here and there we find poems about people as in for instance a poem about a girl who has run away from home because of abuse. She also has poems about her mother's cancer, her daughter's anorexia. And a poem set in Glasgow in the Kibble Palace. A poem that stands out from the rest and fascinates me is 'A Single Arm'. It is rather surrealistic: the arm has an effect on those who see it simply by its existence. It is a macabre event in the world.

But most of the poems are to do with nature, for instance the growing of potatoes, and the world of apples. Each of the poems is very clear without contortion of thought or language. Thus they attract the reader into their world easily.

Her books (this one and *Standing by Thistles*) give an impression of optimism though they can deal with difficult subjects: this is therefore not the optimism of inexperience. She often uses the word "dance". In a poem like 'Tenting' she sees people sleeping rough in rain and in other poems too she is aware of pain. She belongs to the list of doctors who have contributed poetry to the world not least William Carlos Williams who has I think influenced her. He too was open to experience.

I have enjoyed reading her books and wish her good fortune in the future.

Iain Crichton Smith

THE POET'S PRICE / LAUTENSPIELER

Salzburg 96

this is the deal. I came, I sang
Now, the reckoning. You all
know well the cost of living art,
of listening. I do not claim
the sun, the moon, the mountains;
just
the Caravaggio

SHE SAID

VOICES ON WATER

still, after the years, their voices linger, women's voices
sweet above the ferry's thrum; I do not understand it
nor do I remember the women's faces
though I know the song (sometimes the lyrics drown:
            but not the notes
sweet as sung by fresh-cheeked girls
their black hair snaking slender shoulders)

they will be older now, those women; grey
the darkening song
                        thicker, notes unravelling
        the tune no less demanding
the pier as short, the shore
as rich in stone, the boat
as late
            as late

they will be older now

RIVER

my second daughter wants to *be* a river
told me on an afternoon so hot
so blue
      the Ness crawled dryly, glittering where ducks
steeped in the idle stream, heads tucked
as if to weather frost
        'And then,' she said 'I could explore the world
    I'd be a *big* river, broad. I could go anywhere. I
could have ducks *and* swans.'
          And so she might

and trout and salmon, weed
          and pebbles

there might lap calm pools
beneath a willow's shade
still pools, islanded, with crumbling shores
smooth flat shingle carved
(expressly water-carved)
        to skim
surface yet untrounced by wave or trout:
    perhaps
there will be stones
tender stones
        gentle shade
generous to thirsting deer

SHE SAID

'We must have this river'
rushing down the bank
towards the cool green water
(salt and copper painted)
into which she sank
a thin glass phial, bent
to ease a rubber stopper
in its mouth

loath to seem
confused, I asked
'What's that?' They both
replied 'A soil sampling kit'
as if I should have known;
marked the clear glass 'Salzach'
raised it high, offering pale green froth
to pure blue sky

'We collect
those rivers that we share'
he said. 'We have a number now'
He smiled at her: I
did not stare, took
the phial, admired the river-god
trapped inside, aware
of light through glass
                    diffracting

FROZEN FALL

(Fairy Glen 1996)

now
    the fall drops smoothly
in pools that trap and swirl
cool quiet water;
        then
the river hung, confused
cast above twin shining mirrors
thick enough to walk on: ice magnifying,
arcing bushes, welding
tethering hills
        curved
to tease and shine and
          fall

          sl o w l y

                  s
                      l
              o
                          w
             l
                            y

            water's movement
            stilled to land

    as our smiles are

TODAY

buds on the sprawling wood
of last year's briar
have opened into angry green
paired, fissured leaves
                    thundering

HER BLOOD

the river separates: west - cafes, theatre
cathedral spiralling in autumn dark
east - chainstores bind the heart
of our small town, beflowered
and deflowering

breasting the bridge, my daughter at the wheel
I strum the water's murmuring dissent
where black tides dam the flood and
seas run high, moon-high, the delta
all too close, and silting

we ford the concrete, facing north and home
'What's that?' My daughter's voice. I tear my eyes
from tired waves, the thin reflected sighs
of street lights merging, and the dash of green
'What do you mean?'

'Those green lights on the bridge. Too soon
for Christmas.' She nods to where light itches on the tower
red, no, green. I watch her swinging hair
erase shop windows, questioning
'Go round the town again'

*

the night fills Saturday. The streets are primed
with young folk gleaning happiness from stone
and noise and touch: this river-bank, once dense
with churches now spawns night-clubs, Irish pubs

the new, intense religion. Fiddle-struck
girls struggle through slow vodka in the light
that spills in neon green, and neon red
her blood 'What does it mean?' I shake my head

Green **her**, red **blood**: I ask but never find
the reason for this writing on the bridge
reflections breaking on the squirming flood
in tartan mimicry. No, not the image

tourists might expect. Who would address
the river in such terms? Is it a poem?
Art? or lies?
                'Best go.' Light flashes on

her blood
            her blood
                her blood
                    her blood
                        her blood

and Charlie's story rumbles in my head
his saddest story, and I do not know the end

*

'I had this client once. Not in this town
but in my first appointment. We had time
and money then to try, at least. This girl

I knew would not be easy, for she'd come
half-way across the country, left her home
with nothing but the clothes she wore

she wouldn't stay
Twelve, fourteen days, she'd be away
back to her family

Her father's touching frightened
The boyfriend frightened more
She left, trailed home

to labour, late for work
wound the doll in swaddling clothes
laid him on a pillow

*

Her brother told the boss
a crisis called for her at home
Outside the shop
he swore and kicked
and punched
locked her in her room
The baby was not there
'Don't ever even think
of it again' her father said
'We've sorted things'
She stripped the dripping bed
searched in all the drawers
                    searched
every day
Once, she read
about a baby floating on the tide
knew it was her child
A river crept by the estate
She walked there
day in, day out
When it got too hard
she'd sit on littered banks
tranfuse the flood, weeping
from slashed wrists
      We talked
            she cried
as she had never cried
not when they hit or kicked
or swore'

'And then?'
'She never came again
And then I moved
but how can we go on,' he shakes his head
'Wading her blood?'

*

it's grown so dark, so strange
'What are you thinking of?'

My daughter drives beyond the town
too fast

I do not tell her: do not
criticise

lost in the firth, tides
centrifuge our drifting

FOREST

(blackstand farm)

a forest of six thousand oaks
no higher than my thumb
the roots three times the height
each bud a tenth
                    and stretching

                    these tiny silvered
clods of black earth, grown
will keel ships, mast
heart caskets

THE CRETAN LIAR

Tonight I will make summer pudding
as cold winds flatten barley and the swifts
cower in eaves too narrow to support
winged magnificence: it never rains
on our black hill, our barley-covered hill
unwilling gold, near-black with never-rain

Cold wind flattens barley, and the swifts
cower in eaves near-black with never-rain
shunning the wagtail, scorning the red kite
that scour our stringless fields, as I unfold
summer fruits, soft flesh, the dripping sweets
of southern slopes, sun-scathed

and narrow bread
near-black, rain-scathed in eaves
where dipping swift and wagtail do not fly
pressing, spoons my oozing flesh
shout if you dare
All Cretans lie

THIS EXTREME OF WHITE[1]

it has not snowed, not properly:
frost shines on the salted windows
harder to shift
than all your snow

snow falls, and suddenly
but frost snaps silent
on a cloudless world

you lose your footing

[1] *... there is nothing as silent as snow ... all it can ever know is this extreme of white ...* Peter Mortimer

SNOW FALLING

'I always think,'
            she said
'snow is deceitful. Hides
a multitude of sins:
below that white
anything can be
        could be
going on
        Like folk'

Snow fell
    was general
and free of footprints

HOUSE OF BUTTERFLIES

odd to find
     the first day of the year
torn butterfly wings on the stone floor
of the cooling kitchen, two fragments only
yellow, streaked with blue,
ink-blots of black with perfect rounded edges:
I scoop the fragments, crush them

    later I wonder
if I have imagined wings
but others too have seen them
      have assumed
a grubbing chrysalis mistook New Year for summer
I am not so sure
though it is true our windows
are encrusted with cocoons; unseasoned
heating might confuse the issue

    and then
to pass the house above the bay
the empty house, its windows sharded
all the stained glass gone
the storm door limping open
      That house must fall
and soon. Even three years ago
it seemed so strong and whole

      Tom
says it still holds chairs and beds
table, dishes too; even the cutlery
lies restless in rough dresser drawers
a pie-dish courts the chipped white sink
the oven, slick with grease
breeds unwashed pans

and round the scattered windows
in cracks about the cornices
cauling ceiling roses where the wires
flail unlit, the dull cocoons
cling rigid till summer:
the chance of wings, of fresh blood
pumping new horizons, flight
the chill of nectar

   flight
       the chill of nectar

   three years ago this house seemed
good and strong

A SINGLE ARM

the severed arm
lay in sweet grass, wondering
what next to do

first it had scared the tinkers
and then the fair-haired woman
without even a twitch
just by being there!

next it glared at uniformed police
did not say anything
no lawyer present, no telephone call
and no-one asking anyone's permission
for photographs

the arm glared
no-one blinked an eyelid
'No-one missing,' mused the cop
'No other body parts?'
They shook their heads
they'd all been disappointed
but would not be that night
the arm grinned
it would see them all at midnight
                              it
would slink in all their beds
as they slept fitfully, without permission
no, it
            would not leave them

wherever the policeman threw
disjointed bone, the arm
would yearn in grass, a sweet burn
bubbling yards away
                              taut fingers scouring
earth that did not sooth

or dance indifferently
                    in rooms unqualified
arriving suddenly in schools, in hospitals, in
restaurants
           sliming hot car seats, its chill
decaying days, erupting darkness

it
    would never leave them

not a single one of them

STRANGE TOWERS

I have walked in cities where they write on walls
to outface time and lack of money: brick
unsoftened by a tree except where bushes cling
to uncleaned rones, or sprout from cracks
in parting wall
I have walked in cities, longed for light
walked in safe places only

to shops and cafes, in the busier parks
through Glasgow washed with constant rain
(and no umbrella)
I have walked, effacing others' light
in paint or marble, have not
wandered canal banks
to your strange towers, pigeon lofts

enduring where the people flew

(THE MOON)

LIKE SILVER

what colour did we call the moon
before Sappho told
of its silver
rose-like fingers?
(white roses; white roses)

was the moon
a butterball?
did Greeks
eat cheese? or did they
just run Marathons
slurping yoghurt?

Greek skies
were grey; Greek skies
were never blue
there was no word
for it

what colour
was moonlight?

IN THE KIBBLE PALACE: SUNDAY MORNING

Old men on benches outstare tired marble
the rippling misery of one distressed
Adonis carved in mid-sigh, tortuous
among chrysanthemums. His head is bowed.
Perhaps he is allergic to chrysanthemums, wishes
to stroll the Systematic Garden
                    the Border Chronological
                              the Arboretum?
Old men know better. Huddled in damp warmth
this early Sunday morning, they have braved the wind
and found it wanting

The glass roof curves in onion splendour
green as unpicked fruit; light struggles
to diffuse through panes as thick
with mould as glass, swims greenly over foliage
preying on deep-sea lack of rays. No fish
fly here; a noisy sparrow shoals
I walk the gravel gravely
Behind me, children shout, escape into the inner swell
of palm and fern and moss, a green confusion
curdling frantic orders from the tired mother
stuck with the push-chair on the dripping stone
unable to pursue the restless feet that prowl
the quiet inner jungle

Statues are strange, the skin as smooth
the arms and legs and hair
as full and free as if each figure breathed
caught in the endless moment of our choosing
and yet the eyes are empty:
                              do not choose the eyes
the fate that tempts those eyes. Pass on to note
the curling hair, the twisting abdomen
the torso thinned implausibly, the bending knees
the veined arms straining still to grip the marble base

or choose the toe
pointing towards the stone, the frozen stone
the next step over frozen water: choose that early moment
the child now bent on forward movement
without forward bias, her strength still all behind
the weight, the safety all behind: and yet the child intent
on forward movement
                 Choose that moment, note how heavily
the sheltering rock is built behind the child, not moving yet
set on a course as free as lack of movement
and all her strength so much behind

your child, your own child, pale as marble
weak as water on a split palm leaf; your own child
weaker than the water, set on movement
set on a forward course beyond the palms
and all her strength behind
               No due momentum
without clear support, and you intent
on forward movement, lost in outer green
stranded on rain-damp stone

The jungle lives and breathes in glass. Without
the soaring skin, without this constant heat, the leaves
would die, the statues mimic catholic cemeteries
Italian marble, winged, the frozen smile
the sepia photograph
               This jungle lives:
children hide and seek within its heart
Old men stare down visitors

I BIND MY HEART

(to paper mast)

floating is a careful
art, necessary where feet
refute firm land

WALKING NAKED

i

and if
     they make your pain a poem
who could deny it? Or patent such a rhythm
sharp-edged? Ice
               on winter fingers, thinned
to light, night a stretching terror
from knowing to unknowing: in your fear
you feed us all

          and we walk with you
naked

ii

RIDDLED

the ward is quiet: most visitors long gone
Yellow curtains flutter in the draught
the open window stuck, impossible to close
                      I know. I've tried
and standing on this seventh storey sill
is not my favourite angle

My mother died in this ward
no, she didn't
but this was where we faced white shadows
The junior doctor mumbling, waved the Chest Xray
'Riddled with it.' As she spoke
I noted white shoes, matching white coat, saw
how right they were. I
                          never thought of white

I never thought of you
in this white bed

iii

PERSEPHONE

there must bleed a myth along these lines
the child who starves and stares and disappears
smiling at death's closed eyes

refusing wine and bread, refusing mead
refusing sleep, refuting warmth - a child
who stares and starves, then disappears

quietly, her vanishing distress no longer luminous
stretching to infinity, a breath
mythical as any Greek perspective

iv

FORFEIT

always you demanded Pass the Parcel
sellotaped the layers, forfeits too
creased the blackening newsprint
only the first and last
sheets birthday-wrapped (we used
      used paper even then)

     layers counted
music primed

I hand it to you. This is one
I'd never have predicted, nor, I think
would you; the wrinkled skins
shed wearily, green birthday jelly
caking forfeit floor, where we observe
and pass

      the music quickening
as layers fall

v

MIRRORS

        must be outfaced
easier to fix
an eye on shapeless light
or silhouette
sleek passing wall
the undisturbing gift
of lack of light

bones stretch where skin
would slide, bones hang
bones illustrate the frame
bones limber
tenting resonance
bones linger as the skin
settling to bone
slips wry, intense

bones silver
startling sinews

vi

BREAD FOR BOBBIE SANDS

you tell me on the phone you dreamed
of languishing in prison, scratching walls
and even when you woke, the dream
remained - the clothes, the smell. You
could not leave the prison, could not free
yourself, and no-one paid your bail

and did you think of Bobbie Sands?
How old were you
when he starved painfully to prison death?
The news upset you (were you two?
Were you three?) Did you
think of Bobbie Sands last night? You wanted
to send bread for Bobbie Sands: I said
it wouldn't get there, that he wouldn't eat it
if it did

you know that too, this hunger strike
almost as successful. Still
the pain, the rationale
collude:
        the will to die as strong
in any of us. Fuck
the world. Who needs to eat
where thirst, where hunger fuel?

BEFORE A RISING MOON

listen, I will paint you a world
you *will* want to inhabit, where the walls
dissolve in air and trees, the sweet night
sudden with stars, before a rising moon

Far off, a dog barks, far off down the hill
below the Seven Sisters, below Orion's heel
below the sharp point of his sword, below the
reddening star, the dog barks, and complaining

fills our dark hill and the sky; and still
we walk in early frost, disparate footsteps
more substantial, firmer, in the tender dark:
you and I, walking

If we were to talk, we'd miss the absent wind
the gentler breath of sheep and cattle grazing behind wire
wished away: we'd miss the trail of shooting
stars, our eyes fixed on the stars to fasten meteor showers

you and I, walking
as we have always walked

Between this moment and the pain
tired confusion
roses die in winter, but the thorn

stays relevant: thorns snatch
even our dead thorns snatch
though petals never linger, and the hip

scourged red, will pale in withering frost;
roses die in winter, wait
for spring

If it were dawn, we would not have the stars
if it were dawn, prayer would not amplify
if it were dawn, the grey world would demand our tears
if it were dawn, the wires, the walls would rise
if it were dawn

we share
        the stars' dark freedom
crushed and sudden

BRIEF ENCOUNTER

AVAILABLE LIGHT

Eve Arnold said that someone
told her 'If you are not good
enough, you're not close enough'
we are not close

enough to say with Williams
'the business of love
is cruelty, which.. we transform
to live together'

           February slides
I ache for goodness
               light

CLAPPING RHYMES

harder to keep hands in order
than remember rhyme

I had not noticed
hands so suddenly
no longer rounded, fingers
almost elegant, as when
her baby-muscled
hands were disconcerting
(elongated hands
                        incapable
of more than random
movement)

            hands
less feckless now
still inarticulate:

dependent on the rhyme

TORCHING CELLULITE

In the department store
a varnished floor
effaces the cosmetic customer
cheeks delicately powdered
    eyes confused
implicit structure boned and blushed
in pristine nylon
and hypoallergenic smudge-free lash
beyond the fragranced counter

Where do they find these girls?
Where do they find
the slim magnificence
the height of heel
maintained from nine to five
(till eight on Thursdays)
refusing varicosity
support hose banned
complexion toned
to each new season's vagaries?

Not in the customers
    not in the few
who lie in facial reverence
    and buy
the book of beauty (now reduced)
    and buy
the face-wash, toner, base, foundation, buy
the blush
conditioner
    eye-shadow
    liner
mascara
lipstick
    eye-make-up- remover
    the night-cream, wrinkle-cream

the magic cream
for torching cellulite;

      not in these few
the cool-eyed, close-masked
girls who float and sell
cosmetic dreams
at new inflated prices

No, not mere customers
these amazons: ice-maidens
drenched in lily, abdomens
exhumed, refilled
with meadow-grass and flowers
all beauty purchased
weapons slung at hip
in ritual display
the powder-shield, mascara lance
(eyes plucked out at root
and flowers and civet strewn
or rubbed
in due proportion:
      brain
seeps fluid from the skull
into the cooling
years)

skin
    may outlast myth-maker
and myth
    cling to bone, the withering fruit
of apple-picking youth
but in the store, myth
matters:
we fill the skull
with flowers

CROPMARKS

Only in a good year
only when the sun
shines long and hot and true
will you see
the hidden perfect ditches
rampart remnants, drains
where love once ran, outcropping
silting years

BRIEF ENCOUNTER

Why does that stewardess call up the faded photos
of my mother's war-time friends?
The hair straw-bleached (incongruous in Stornoway)
strafing business huddles, thin men, thirty-something
fumbling lap-tops, mobile phones
(fashionable in Glasgow too)

Who needs these toys? Not
our stewardess, humming as she pours her tea, sips
absent-minded

Is it the hair, scrawled back, too neat
bleach extending briefly to darkening roots
that better suit her skin? Red lipstick coats full lips
round, curving lips and cup; a cigarette
held with flamboyant grace, the stretched hand
trailing smoke dreams, helical, too far away
for smell to foul the picture

She cannot smoke on board. Perhaps
she is addicted, has waited all day
for this consummation: or
she may think it graceful, like my mother's friends
who all smoke languidly in smiling
photographs

What else did you do
*   with hands left idle?*

The captain hovers, stiff in peaked cap, heavy
braid. Is that the key? The uniform? My
mother's snaps drip uniform, the girls
recline in uniform, too big, too small,
unlike our stewardess, whose tailored blue
fits where the WAF shirts didn't

does uniform evoke those days, delays
at Crewe with kitbag, like our delay in Stornoway
this restless end of day, connections crossed
in thickening dusk? Or is
her face old-fashioned, eyes too close
for nineties' beauty?

THE BIG ONE

the security man
checks luggage briefly
his unwilling fingers
dip and delve in private places
(x-rays would be better)
wishes he were on the loch
a late mist, hip flask rising

in the delay
he makes a call

'Did you clean that fish?
The big one?'

NO STARS TONIGHT

no stars tonight
the wind
blew snowless
paring skin and bone
no moon

I blame
the cutbacks

I TRACE YOUR NAME

LINGERING WOOD

once I got it home, the fine white cotton
seemed no longer old, the buttons new
generous length too much for just a night-gown: I
had bought (in wistful pride)
              a shroud

  cloth to please a body's sweet decay
in late magnificence, cloth I'd assumed
enticed, repelling
              every tender death
a possibility, the body's melding flesh to bone
a certain understatement, courting probability

  cloth deters. Unfleshed, my ravelling fingers
pall decaying breast, ribs flailing under ironed frills

  do shrouds endure
              in lingering wood?

THESE QUIET NIGHTS

these quiet nights
                the owls
haunt every tree around this garden
most of all the oak; we never see them
from their contralto lyric
assume the varying platform
   (I say contralto, never having prized
the simpler coloratura
lower than the blackbird
softer than the crows
that choir our daily scattering)

we do not feed the owls

neither do we nail them
above the door, relying
on rowan leaves to ward off black intent
or rowan branches, bare
to blind the evil eye, dampen
sightless song: our winter owls
fly freely in the garden

do not sing of death

but at the year's bleak turn
I scathed a white owl on the road
beyond Munlochy wood, the black sky
fading, the bitter morning clenched
the dawn too weak to sing
ice blown stark on field and stone

a hunting owl
rising from the kill
  I could not brake
on ice, I could not brake
  my heart flew forward

silvered tar, the owl dance
feathering

we do not savour impact
cannot waive the ice, the rowan pale
the hard year seeding death's waxed frame
we do not weep for owls who plane
the night's insistence, beak and talons
honed, eyes everywhere:

we do not paint the owl
as victim

THE APPLE FALLS

the apple falls, ripening
cannot be gently prized from
twig and branch till weight and sap
release the seed-trap
            tempting
Eves, birds, aphid Snow-whites

(they avoid the red cheek)

TENTING

the campers by the beach cannot be sleeping, surely
not in drumming rain, the hills and seas
a merging of incongruence, each burn a squall
of angry threatening: new pastures, paths

the campers by the beach should all have gone
if they had sense, quit the filling sea, the spoiling dolphins
fleeing nylon tunnels (sober-green) thick wheeled bikes
with multiple panniers (too rough, too bulky)

the campers should be wrapped in bed and breakfast houses
safe in warming towels, cannot all
be sleeping. No, I cannot see them sleeping, not
in fettered rain

A strange space, tunneled nylon, even in good weather
the inner cotton tent a wafting damp
of flies, wet ground too hard to lie on, walls too narrow
roof too low to sit

within this space you crawl as in bleak Japanese hotels
coffin-like hotels, where space is no
illusion, no constraint, but absent, one cubed metre
of concern and claustrophobia

(the tent is voluntary: the rain
is voluntary)

lying in strange space you reach out, lying
in pale narrowness, the walls a folding grief, the roof a net
filtering the sealing rain; you reach in cloying vacuum
to lack of visibility, to rain
that leavens rooms you might have left, rooms
you might have lived
                    in soft green light

THERE IS

there is always, the sea
the moaning sand, the waves impermanent
the tickling, drenching weed

and then the shells
                        swimming, broken, dead
for our delight, for our
confusion, for shell boxes, shell-
sand

(shell-sand clings where true sand falls
stings as it dries on warm flesh, stings
where true sand itches: water does not
ease such company)

still there is always water
always salt

I TRACE YOUR NAME

in sand before
the water's edge; whether the spell
will take, I cannot tell
the tide
being neither out nor in
clear direction hard to fathom

the dark sand wet and firm
my finger drawing sure resistance
sand-flies, shells, a small stone
dark and smooth:

I cannot read
you at this distance, cannot waive
the sand
stray letters swirling
tidal waters

THE PERFECT MOMENT

I cannot bear to think how your fleshed bones
endure the frost, the patchy
turf and wreaths
    you
who could never bear the cold
would never dance
did not learn early, did not
lie
 encouraged dancing
in us, charged our feet
with lightness and a love
of your lost youth:

I feel you turning
     as
his whistle sharpens towelled ears
the rough wool of your dressing gown
damp against wet skin
conscious of your sudden breast
the danger of wet thigh
slipping from safe harbour, parting
wool from hip to thigh

I feel you turning, flushed
your nipples startled, feel you turn
altering your step
to gain the corner's safety
flushed, the wash-bag
jangling hurried thigh

you
 turning

you who never learned
to dance
  or lie

THE PERFECT MOMENT

all dancers seek this: and you
are a dancer, carry clothes
with care, move with a pride
an energy not obvious till sought

I see you in the distance, down
the long white corridor, would call
your name, but caught by movement
let the moment pass

your hand upon the stair, the curving
stair, your gentle hand
not touching, quite, the rail
as you assume descent

I watch this perfect moment, ache
to call, to touch you

THE PERFECT MOMENT

always, the hesitation
perfection of unknown intent
unrecognized, unfelt
the joy of bones, unruly

salt sea rising
over safer walls
that may endure
or fall

ANGEL GRAVESTONES

ANGEL GRAVESTONES

to find

    after the storm
        this peace in mood and weather

a littered beach
        divining sea and cliff
the waterfall
        exploding
carving sand, deepening

the shallow channel
        temporary
no less transient

        this Sunday morning

lends more faith
        than angel gravestones

WHEATEAR

I want to know the names of all the birds
that sing about our fences:
sparrows, more or less
with subtle differences

move too fast for me to mark the shape
the colour of the tail
they all have wings, fly
dipping, wheel

above, below our tiled roof
penetrate the eaves
sing from the chimney
scurry in the waves

of barley stubble, mouse-like:
when the plough
scars the rising field
they know

enough to leave the pickings
to larger birds
seagulls, crows
that swerve:

they are not tits and chaffinches
these smaller creatures
neither by note
nor feather

POTATOES

never flourished in our garden, but even
when her leg shrunk, Mattie grew them, weed-free
in much polished drills
                              Eddie too, his breath
a whisky stour, his garden preened, fat petunias
hiving the velvet lawn, while at the back potatoes
put forth creamy flowers:
their gardens separated by a single block
 ours a street and field away, untidy
(My parents were not gardeners, nor am I
nor am I a cook)
                        We never grew potatoes,
almost never, but if a neighbour brought some,
Eddie came, or Mattie sent a bag
                                       we'd wish
we had, wish we'd bent our backs
to hoe the endless pyramids where rough grass
toughed out summers, rarely mown

This knife is blunt. My mother used to sharpen knives
against the squat fat step. If tinkers came
they'd get the work of grinding smooth and sharp
the dulled edge (they came for rags more often
than they came for work)
                              She would always welcome them
always kept a rag in case the tinkers came

This knife is blunt. I force it through soft flesh
that should be firm and is not, force it
Still the tinkers do not come

Now potato fields, tractor-fed, forced and fertilised
bloom till autumn when the vibrant shaws
are weed-killed, and the stench of withering
would make you weep
                           Those plants feel pain, you know this

73

even as you drive, windows tightly shut
against the seeping:
you know this as you peel

the knife cuts rough, startling whiteness

ARCHAEOLOGISTS

who are they
that sift the desert sand
for bone with sinew
still attached, full heads of hair
thrown roughly to one side
by early looters?

much remains
too much in sand, too human
too visible and ancestor:
how do those fragments smell?

pictures hide the smell

odd that skin should cling
so long

RODDY'S MEDAL

He was good at school, a sure high flier. Here's
the medal in its leather case; silver-gilt
wreathed in fern and daisies *for Excellence
in Classics 1938 Tain Royal Academy.*
In 1942 his solo flight fuelled fern and daisies
on a hill not fifty miles from home; his brothers
missing - Willie in the desert, Gregor off to Africa
with bride. They died, the ship sunk, life-boats
strafed in missionary zeal. The telegram that told
the tale was lost, funding further harsh
mythology; for as we wept for one son
drowned in air, newspapers tolled Ocean Tragedy

WE DO NOT TENDER SPANISH COIN:

                                        the
coins chink, restless
in roving fingers, small coins, worn with age
tired gold
          no longer pure

gold cannot bind the years, gold does not shine
in sweat and dark: gold glancing gold
does not excite, though gold in sun
convinces, warming

love
     will we seek the sun, the tarnished hoard diminishing
gold spent in skin? Or will we cling
to coin, to nervous movement, the dark disablement
of careful years

               our fingers restless, hearts
unrisking

Anne MacLeod

THE CERTAINTY OF ICE

there is in this coolness
the certainty of ice:
it melts

come, my white love
sing
spring shocks us

sing, my white love
                    come

WAS IT MUSIC?

the road is narrow to the former church
not single track, still wide enough
to quell opposing traffic: west and south
it wavers in lost green, the leafy wood
feathering a green scene out of Constable
or painted back-drop, Arden (Macbeth
country here pleads Arden
lacks the sheer descent to Birnam
in this green, this narrow rendering)

low scooped hills creep from the wood
and shrouding corner, wreath
a fine square building with no sign
of graveyard; white church, squat manse
unadorned by gravestones (chimney pots
support the crumbling wall, stand stiffly
mourning houses, hearths
                              decayed)

inside no light
                there never was
the lack of stained glass testifies, the lack
of glass, and no space
            quiet damp perpetuating
sofas, chairs, commodes
penitent tables gathering
communed in presence of the worm
of possibility of judgement
where the mark that separates
the lost from possible, good from used
is mere belief

we tender preying eyes
on congregations
weigh the grace of chairs, bare rugs
the sweet decay of trunks

(where have they been? Whose clothes
lay folded here?)
Sometimes we buy, sometimes we turn
affirming the green road
though wardrobes offer real temptation
army coats and tails; that dressing gown
of cloth of gold, moth-savoured wedding dresses
hung by flannel nightgowns
(resolutely wide)

there is no music now: no precentor preens
a flagging congregation where each note
is stretched for longer than seems likely
longer than the neighbouring note, louder too
the tune improbable
            or unimportant
there is no music, no, nor sermon
pulpits long replaced
the odd stray pew not integral, but bought
(another church, defrocked
enduring like decay)
there is no music

      was it music?

AFTER THE DARK

after the cleansing dark
I want to drink the light
to drown in it
throw curtains wide
slit blinds
assume the wide wide sky
the plateau strung from sea to mountains
thickening shifting cloud
unable to defuse the bellowing
light

POYNTZFIELD

we climb the wooden stair right to the top
soothe the gentle ghost drifting idle in the west wing
pass the endless snooker table, dining table longer
than most houses, all the bathrooms now en-suite
(the damp is slight, the floor bare wood, dark-stained;
starred curtains rise)
                              We climb the tower
shielded by lead roof and height
lost to all eyes below the dome
where you stand naked

it takes a high roof and a steady mind to bear
such attitude in bronze
too small a house would falter:
to know and always know
                              the chorus stark
beneath sleek posturing would sour mythology
impose a different story

                    *

birds settle on the upturned breast, gentler than
bruised hands that brush the nipple roughly
flexing outstretched arms:
                              birds settle and their claws
bite as you turn, chaste as moonlight
one breast a seagull's perch, the other festering in years
reliving mould calm hands wrought
                                        skin withdrawn

birds settle
wind absolves their clamour

                    *

and still the beat of hands discovering shape, bronze shape
enduring sun and rain
                        exposed, insisted
open to the world
                        the seeing eye moves hands
to shape obscurity in bronze
                                where shaping hands obscure

we climb the stair
the wind
            absolves our clamour

THE GREEN FIG AT THE DOOR

my youngest daughter swarms
in fig-thin branching by the door, beleafed
but only just: this year there will be two or three
where last year we took seven figs
(perhaps the harder winter, sharper
spring?)
        She does not care, bare
shoulders parching leaves
that blister light-drenched skin
I call
        She will not hear

burrowing kitchen heat, the eldest
dreams of figs, sweet and firm, flesh
tempting fading skin:
our small green northern fig
no less desirable than southern fruit
the flesh as rich, the stone
as firm
        She will not bite
her bones serene in emptiness. Replete
she will not eat

the last child, swathing
golden hair. Our green fig at the door
has yet no meaning for her
not a single flower
snatches winded light in leaves
interminable
        Unconsumed, her dreams
are not of figs, but
pointed toes, stiff lace, sword-
dancing

IT STARTED WITH APPLES

it started with apples drying in the loft
over winter: why some rotted, others dried

on festering wood he could not say, yielding
flesh smelled yet as sweet

as rose-oil girls decanted on slim wrists
on Saturdays before the early dance

or Sunday church, the same smell
fingering

rough beams splintered searching fingers, apples too
picked fruit on newsprint thickly spread

each vibrant corpse a universe, and they
ripe flesh-devourers, shriking scarlet larders

winter all the paler as fruit decayed
grey spores spiked skin and wood:

each fall he stole an apple
laid it in calm dust below his bed

each year saw apple swell
to bitter core, mice needle perfect skin;

each year he plucked one apple
braved the din, the apple shrieking

the girl my mother chose smelled apple/rose
thin wrists did not entice but she
proved strong enough: we filled the loft
draping beams with thyme
the floor a tide of apples: I killed

pheasants, pigeons; once, a swan
each with a single stroke, one stone
she hung them in the barn

I stalked, grew clever, seeking harder fare:
she upbraided me for choosing larks
Larks should scour the skies, she cried
And swifts? Too acrobatic
Buzzards? Cruel
I tossed them at her feet, thin feet
she swung them, feathered, dripping
over lofted apples

and no-one ate, no-one
ate the lark, the buzzard: no-one ate
the feathered ripening
I sulked, grew bolder, seeking different fare

his mother's dead flesh cooled as fast
as stone-killed birds

his mother who had never
slept an hour

beyond the dawn lay stiff and white
candling slow surprise

that death should find in her
a fully able victim:

her flesh, like other flesh
invoking earth and flame

no leathered pelt, no saint
in cool cathedral

his mother's flesh
            he could not save

but in the loft, contrite with apples
other flesh, fruit of my concern, endures
I scour cold entrails, carving wood to ease
what gapes below
the cloak of feathers each bird
sings to fill

the wood as sweet as roses
apple-wood as sweet, sweeter
than the bright lark's soaring

she does not understand
the girl his mother chose

does not understand
the single slit

from beak to tail, the easing
of the lifeless into endless shape

beyond life, saving feathers'
swift cohesion

she does not understand
she rocks her son

as I wire beak and wing

BLACKSTAND

what I do not know
    is where they found the paint: I
saw the images in wavering light, the thin
tattooing torch-stream danced, and in its fingering
shocked leaves where full white breasts escape
the lime-wash;
           this is what I saw, white-wash
paling shimmering light (dreams
wrought fifty years before that light)
      paint
         I saw the paint wrought light
in dreaming

     and walking where they walked
from the hut beside the wood
(were there trees in those days? On
an airfield?)
      walking where they walked
along the narrow lane, whin and gorse
relieving gun and wire
walking where they walked
towards the steading, still I wonder
how it started

     next to their cinema, this long, low loft:
a place of dreams, of light in flickering life, a place
where fliers surfaced from cold air, submerging fear
and hope in new mythology, the light
no clearer than the sun they chased in gun and wire
along the narrow tarmac;
          in this loft
they slept and dreamed, bare-walled
before the paint, before the brothers dreamed
      before
the brothers

the space now cluttered; fifty years'
degenerate confusion, cots and beds
old cookers, years, decades
                    decanting damply,
                            dreams discounted
(trees soar where the hangars stood, trees
bind torn earth where fliers
scratched brief landings safer fields
refused)
            full fifty years of dust
and still the paint clings roundly to bare skin
refuting white concealment
                    the brothers' leaves
outlive celluloid, the screen-wall's gabling
names unknown

        I wonder
                at brothers being cast
together on an airfield so remote, still
they were brothers; straggling veterans
attest, visiting the farm purely to view
remembered scenes, these walls
the frescoed cinema
a place of dying pilgrimage, Blackstand:

    it has been several years now
since one came

                *

    some, perhaps, were desolate to find
walls dashed with lime, save
one clear panel on the right
where swords clash, velvet cavaliers
spill lace, black curls
(their reasonable horses
pawing river banks
in summer shade)
the action more convincing
at a distance

and on the left, cross-bearing
Christ tempts a thin blue veil
from bare-breasted Veronica
(this too escaped the censor
where Adam's perfect frame
did not, nor Eve's
despite the proffered apple;
of the serpent, no trace
whoever scraped the whitewash
did not resurrect
the snake)

the walls had other tales to tell
those fliers knew
came in drifts to chip concealing paint
scarify the curtaining white
the fliers peeled
surface and the substance to receding
skin

*

did they cajole a Black Isle girl
to pose red-nippled, light the nights
of eager, lonely boys?
                        Or did they flesh
foreshortening in rosy dreams
(paint diverting fuselage
to corsage, Myrna Loy
in poster-definition?)

            faces
never change, flesh breathes
within arms' reach
perspective less than simple
(never simple)
                it took
a seeing eye to place that paint
it took an eye

and practice; unexpected depth
and height:

the naked girl with lover
        that green girl on the bed
whose dress spills open to the waist
        Veronica and Eve
the mother and her infant
share one face
                one expression
the half-dream/ smile
                        the action (lack
of action)

                *

    where does their passion end? designed
to ease a lonely hour, tender warmth

from wind (a wind which did not
. understand it, fettered by the trees

the winter fir and larch) brush-strokes stir
thin light they do not understand:

as fliers strafe the sun, their swords, their
pale, deliberate horses

pawing gentle shade, the action
more convincing at a distance:

                brothers' shades
requiting narrative

TOUCHING

such a simple thing, the pressure
arm on arm, cloth on cloth
the softnesses, the strength
bone and sinew and sun;
and sun and early morning dew
rising on the meadow
in sweet white mist
grass weeping
weeping

NOTES

11. The poet's price: the ancient Celtic bards could name their price and get it; those who failed to pay (or insulted the poet) ran the risk of having a satire composed against them, which was greatly feared.

    Lautenspieler: Caravaggio's 'Lute Player' in the Residenz Art Gallery, Salzburg

25. The old joke - "All Cretans are liars. I'm a Cretan, I should know."

26. "... there is nothing as silent as snow / and all it can ever know / is this extreme of white ..." Peter Mortimer: 'The extreme of white'. *A rainbow in its throat*, Flambard, 1993: 26-27.

32. Doocots, Union Canal, Glasgow

33. Sappho was the first person to call the moon silver. In another fragment the moon is "rose-fingered, after the sun has set". Sappho: *Poems and Fragments*, Bloodaxe, 1992.

34. The Kibble Palace, with its fine collection of marble statues by Hamo Thornycroft and Goscombe John, is one of the large hothouses in Glasgow's Botanic Gardens.

42. Bobbie Sands: an IRA prisoner who died on hunger strike in 1981.

47. Eve Arnold, photographer, famous for using available light only.

    William Carlos Williams, American poet, "The business of love is / cruelty, which / by our wills, / we transform / to live together" 'The Ivy Crown'. *Selected Poems*, Penguin, 1976: 189-191.

49. In the last few years Russian archaelogists have unearthed frozen intact remains of Altai tribeswomen buried with their weapons and horses two thousand years ago, the intricate rituals of preparation of the body after death still clear.

51. Cropmarks - variations in crop-growth caused by deeply buried ditches or foundations.

77. In the course of a Spanish wedding ceremony the bride and groom exchange twelve gold coins to ensure long-lasting prosperity.

82. Poyntzfield, on the Black Isle, is a fine Georgian house, topped by an octagonal cupola on which shines the bronze naked statue of a previous owner.

85. I am grateful to the young Spanish colleague who told me of the house in Rioja which used to belong to her grandfather. He had killed (with a sling shot) one of each of all the local birds of prey, and taught himself taxidermy to preserve them in a room adjoining the house, where they still are. The poem is not about this particular family, though I have adopted the haunting image of the bird collection.

Celtic shamen and poets wore feathered cloaks (song-birds) as part of their regalia, often trimmed with the head and neck of a swan.